MW00954656

INSTANT POT COOKBOOK: 100 HAND-PICKED RECIPES FOR YOUR ELECTRIC PRESSURE COOKER

COPYRIGHT 2018_Messiah Sanders

All rights reserved. No part of this book can be reproduced, distributed or transmitted in any form or by any means including print, electronic, scanning or photocopying unless prior written permission is granted by the author or publisher.

Table of Contents

CHAPTER 4: RICE, BEANS & LENTIL INSTANT POT RECIPES

Vegan Pudding

Cilantro Peas Rice

Mushroom risotto

CHAPTER 5: MOUTHWATERING INSTANT POT DESSERTS

Apple Sauce

Rice Dessert

Baked Apples

Sugar-free Caramel Sauce

Vegan Rice Pudding

Strawberry Jam

Tapioca Pudding

Oats and Coconut Milk Kheer

Red Bean Rice Cake

Vegan Lemon Cheesecake

Vegan Coconut Yogurt

Poached Pears

Paleo Rosemary Applesauce

Chai Rice Pudding

Orange Spice Cake

Apple Cranberry Crisp

Apple and Lavender Cake

Blueberry Mug Cake

Chocolate Chip Raspberry Mug Cake

Apple Cinnamon Mug Cake

Banana Chocolate Mug Cake

Almond Carrot Cake

Almond Coconut Cake

Almond Cheesecake

Walnut Dark Chocolate Cake

Thai Coconut Custard

Chocolate Chip Pumpkin Cake

Avocado Banana Plantain Cake

Pumpkin Pudding

Chocolate Pudding Cake

Biscuit Yogurt Cake

Vanilla Cheesecake

Apple Crisp

Three-layered Chocolate Cheesecake

Chocolate Lava Cake

Caramel Popcorn

Chocolate Mousse

Brown Biscuit Bread

Peach Cake

Lemon Pie

Pumpkin Pie

INTRODUCTION

Throughout the recent years you could have heard already about the Instant Pot, a multi-function cooker. This small device will help you in the kitchen in so many ways, replacing the slow cooker, pressure cooker, steamer, and several other kitchen gadgets. This can help you save some hard-earned money and also contribute to saving some space in the kitchen, since you won't need any other appliances anymore. You should be surprised how this wonder pot can do so many things. Sounds like a miracle to own, isn't it? YES! Instant Pot is capable to become your best friend when it comes to cooking.

HOW DOES INSTANT POT WORK?

If you feel that this wonder appliance fits into your kitchen, then you will be relying on the many functions it includes. There are various models available in the market, so it depends on one's preference to buy a particular model. Most of the Instant Pot models include functions- warming, slow cooking, pressure cooking, yogurt making, streamer, cake maker etc.

For example, when it comes to baking, depending on the model, you can place the cupcake molds or cake trays directly inside the cooker, and let it bake you a perfect dessert.

In addition, the Instant Pot has various functions where you can adjust cooking times and pressure from low to high.

BENEFITS OF INSTANT POT

❖ Practical or suitable cooking
❖ Smart Functioning
❖ Pre-Programmed Cooking
❖ Time saving
❖ Maintains nutrients & cooks delicious food.

PRACTICAL OR SUITABLE COOKING

This miracle pot offers the main operational functions, present right on the front wall of the pot, which makes it very convenient to choose and select between the different functions, such as:

- Multigrain cooking
- Rice cooking
- Porridge
- Soups

- Slow cooking
- Steaming
- Yogurt
- Meat/chili
- Poultry
- Keep warm

The above features help cook the food evenly keeping all the nutrients intact and planning your meals becomes easier too as the cooking time is already set automatically in most of the programs.

SMART FUNCTIONING

All the functions available in every Instant Pot model contribute to the less stressful, automatically-controlled cooking, where the cooking time has been adjusted based on the multiple tests and research to guarantee each meal is thoroughly cooked through and ready to be served when the cooking time is over.

For example- if you are making a porridge- there are multiple stages involved in cooking the porridge and the device is designed in a such a way that the heat is evenly passed throughout all the ingredients.

PRE-PROGRAMMED COOKING

Instant Pot is designed to offer maximum user's convenience. All the functions have pre-programmed cooking times and pressure levels which are set on automatically once you add all the ingredients. You do not have to manually calculate the time or set the time for each stage of cooking. This makes your cooking experience more satisfying and hassle-free.

In addition, once the cooking is done, the device goes to keep warm mode to keep your meal warm and ready to be enjoyed any time you would want to.

SAVES TIME & EFFICIENCY

Food is cooked much faster compared to the traditional cooking methods. Normally, Instant Pot saves 70% of cooking time compared to other methods of cooking like pressure cooking, microwave cooking, steaming, boiling etc. So it can well be declared that the usage of Instant Pot is time & is cost effective as well.

MAINTAINS NUTRIENTS & COOKS DELICIOUS FOOD

Frequently, people believe that during the pressure cooking the foods lose all the nutrients because of the high temperature. This is a Myth. The heat is spread out evenly. In addition, when using your Instant Pot, you don't need to use a lot of water, but just a little amount, necessary for the steaming process. Because of this, the nutrients will not be dissolved but will remain intact throughout the entire cooking process. This further helps in retaining the original color and flavor of the ingredients used.

HOW TO CLEAN THE INSTANT POT

Risk-free Dishwasher parts - Stainless steel Inner pot, Instant Pot sealing ring, and steamer rack can be washed effectively in your dishwasher.

Exterior parts - Never dip or submerge the exterior parts of the pot in the water or any other liquid. Just wipe with a damp clean cloth.

Rim- Always try to clean the rim of the pot with a foaming brush.

Inner Pot - Remove the stains using the white vinegar. Vinegar is the best cleaning agent for removing hard stains.

Lid - Wash the lid in the soapy water.

Instant Pot parts - Clean the anti-block shield, steam release valve, condensation collector on a regular basis.

Silicone Sealing Ring - Remove the stains and odors from the sealing rings. A good advice is to buy and keep an extra pair of rings.

Chapter 2: Hearty Instant Pot Soups

Black Bean Soup

Ingredients:

- 1 pound dried black beans (soaked overnight, rinsed and drained)

- 2 tablespoons extra-virgin olive oil

- 1 red onion (large, chopped)

- 1 red bell pepper (chopped)

- 5 garlic cloves (minced)

- 1 teaspoon ground cumin

- 2 teaspoons dried oregano

- 1 teaspoon black pepper

- 1 1/2 teaspoons salt

- 2'1/4 tablespoons sherry vinegar

- 5 cups water

- 3 chopped tomatoes

- 1 avocado (chopped)

- 5 scallions (minced)

- 1/4 cup red wine

Directions:

1. Open your Instant Pot. Select "Sauté" mode and heat 2 tsp Olive oil. Add the chopped onion, red bell pepper, minced garlic, cumin, and oregano.

2. Sauté until the onions are soft and spices are fragrant, for about 4-5 minutes. Add the pre-soaked beans, black pepper, salt, vinegar, red wine and water. Press "Cancel" button.

3. Cover and seal the Instant Pot according to the instructions. Select "Bean/Chili" setting and set the timer for 15 minutes. After the timer beeps press "Cancel" and let the Instant Pot release the pressure. Remove the lid.

4. Pour your soup to the serving bowls and serve hot. Alternatively, blend half of the beans using a hand blender to get a thick consistency. Serve with red onions & scallions.

Lentil Turmeric Soup

Ingredients

- 3 onions (chopped)
- 2 carrots (chopped)
- 3 stalks celery (chopped)
- 1 tablespoon ginger (minced)
- 2 cans full-fat coconut milk
- 2 cups vegetable broth
- A pinch of salt
- 1/2 teaspoon pepper
- 2 teaspoons cumin
- 1 tablespoon turmeric
- 4 cloves garlic (minced)
- 1 cup red lentils
- 4 cups spinach (chopped)
- 1 tablespoon lemon juice
- 2 tablespoons olive oil
- 1 1/2 cups diced tomatoes

Directions:

1. Switch on the Instant Pot and add all the ingredients except for the spinach and lemon juice, then add the lentils on top.
2. Select "Manual" mode and cook on high pressure for 10 minutes.
3. Opt for the natural pressure release after cooking time is over. Natural pressure release takes around 15 minutes.
4. Pour the soup in a large serving bowl.
5. Using "Sauté" mode, pour lemon juice and add spinach. Cook for 3-5 minutes.
6. Add the cooked spinach to the soup and then serve and enjoy the soup.

Plain Lentil Soup

Ingredients

- 1 teaspoon olive oil
- 1 chopped yellow onion
- 3 chopped carrots
- 3 chopped celery ribs
- 3 cloves of minced garlic
- 1 diced potato
- 2 teaspoons of fresh herbs
- 14 ounces diced tomatoes
- 7 cups vegetable broth
- 2 1/2 cups green lentil
- 3 cups sliced kale
- sea salt to the taste
- black pepper to the taste

Directions:

1. Using the "Sauté" function", heat the olive oil. Then add the onion, carrots, and celery and sauté until the vegetables start to soften, for about three minutes. Then add all other ingredients.

2. Close the pot and press the "Cancel" button. Select the "Soup" mode and adjust the time to 35 minutes.

3. When the cooking time is over, opt for the quick pressure release by opening up the pressure valve. Serve the soup hot and Enjoy!

Split Pea Soup

Ingredients

- 1 cup of split peas
- 2 yellow onions
- 3 carrots
- 2 tablespoons olive oil
- ½ teaspoon lemon juice
- 1 teaspoon salt
- 6 cups water

Directions:

1. Chop the onions finely, and peel and chop the carrots in around 2-inch cubes. Add the olive oil to the inner pot of the Instant Pot, then add the veggies, and select the "Sauté" function.

2. Cook the vegetables and stir as needed, for about five minutes, until they turn soft.

3. Drain the split peas, and add them to the Instant Pot along with 6 cups of water.

4. Lock the lid, cancel "Sauté," and select the "Manual" button. Set the timer for 15 minutes.

5. When the timer beeps, let the pressure get released naturally; this would take 10-15 minutes. Open the Instant pot, add salt as needed and a ½ tsp lime juice and stir it once again and serve it with whole-wheat bread.

Vegan Mushroom Soup

Ingredients

- 2 tsp olive oil
- 1 Chopped onions
- 1 Large chopped celery
- 1 large peeled and chopped carrot
- 4 minced garlic cloves
- 8 ounces sliced Crimini mushrooms
- 8 ounces sliced and stem removed shiitake mushrooms
- 1 tsp dried thyme
- 1/2 tsp ground pepper
- 3/4 cup coconut milk
- 4 cups of vegetable broth
- 1/2 tsp salt

Directions:

1. Switch on the Instant Pot and select "Sauté" mode. Add the olive oil, heat it up for a minute and then add the minced garlic, chopped carrots, celery, onions, and Crimini and Shiitake mushrooms. Sauté for about 10 minutes

2. Once they are soft, cancel the "Sauté" mood. Using a hand blender, puree all the sautéed vegetables.

3. Now, select "Soup" mode on the display, add the coconut milk, vegetable broth, thyme, pepper & salt. Mix well and seal the pot. Adjust the cooking time to 20 minutes

4. After the cooking set time is over, opt for the natural pressure release, then open the pot slowly.

5. Garnish the soup with dried thyme and serve warm.

Vegan Lentil Soup

Ingredients

- 2 tsp olive oil
- 1 chopped onion
- 2 chopped green onions
- 4 cloves of minced garlic
- 2 chopped celery ribs
- 1 tsp chopped ginger
- 2 sprigs fresh thyme
- 2 chopped carrots

- 1 diced potato
- 1 diced sweet potato
- 1/4 tsp cayenne pepper
- 1 1/2 tsp salt
- 1 1/2 cups lentils
- 8 cups water
- 1/4 cup coconut milk

Directions:

1. Switch on the Instant Pot, press "Sauté" mode, pour the olive oil and heat it for a minute. Add chopped onion, garlic, green onions, chopped celery, crushed ginger and cook for about 3 minutes stirring constantly.
2. Add the thyme, carrots, diced potatoes, cayenne pepper, salt, lentils, water, and coconut milk. Stir and cook for 2 minutes.
3. Close and seal the Instant Pot and select the "Manual" mode, setting the cooking time for 15 minutes on high pressure.
4. Once the cooking time is over, release the pressure naturally and serve your soup hot.

Turmeric Sweet Potato Soup

Ingredients

- 2 tsp olive oil
- 1 chopped yellow onion
- 1 sliced celery rib
- 5 minced garlic cloves
- 1 tsp paprika
- 1 tsp ground cumin
- 1/2 tsp salt
- Black pepper to taste

- 1/2 tsp red chili flakes
- 1 cup green or any lentils of your choice.
- 1 peeled and diced sweet potato
- 3 1/2 cups low-sodium vegetable broth
- 2 cups water
- 3 small chopped tomatoes
- 4 cups packed spinach leaves

Directions:

1. Switch on the instant pot, select "Sauté" mode, add the olive oil and heat it for a minute, then add the chopped onions, sliced celery, and minced garlic cloves.

2. Sauté for at least 2 minutes. Add paprika, cumin, pepper, red chili flakes, and then pour the low -sodium broth and 2 cups of water.

3. Then add the diced sweet potato, tomatoes and spinach leaves.

4. Finally, add the lentils. Cancel the "Sauté" mode, and select "Soup" mode and set the cooking time to 30 minutes.

5. Allow the pressure to be released naturally once the soup is done, garnish it with dried thyme and enjoy!

Cauliflower & Broccoli Soup

Ingredients

- 1 head cauliflower, florets separated
- 1 small head Broccoli, florets separated
- 1 chopped onion
- ½ sliced red pepper
- 3 cubed baby potatoes
- 3 minced garlic cloves
- ½ tsp curry powder
- ½ tsp cumin powder
- 1 tsp dried thyme
- 1 tsp cayenne pepper
- 3 cups vegetable broth
- 1 1/2 cups coconut milk
- chopped cilantro

Directions:

1. Switch on the Instant Pot, heat some oil using the "Sauté" mode, then add the minced garlic, onions, pepper cauliflower florets, broccoli, potatoes and simmer for a few minutes.
2. Add the curry powder, thyme, cumin powder, and cayenne pepper, mix well and heat for a minute.
3. Then add the vegetable broth and close the lid. Set the Instant Pot to "Soup" mode, and adjust the cooking time to 5 minutes.
4. Once done, release the pressure and carefully open the Instant Pot. Add in the coconut milk and mix gently to combine. Season with salt and pepper. Garnish with fresh chopped cilantro. Enjoy!

Vegan Lentil Vegetable Soup

Ingredients

- 10oz frozen vegetables mix
- 4 large diced
- 14oz white beans
- 10oz soaked kidney beans
- 1/4 cup soaked quinoa
- 1 tsp basil
- 1 tsp minced garlic

- 1 ½ tsp hot red sauce
- 1/2 tsp oregano
- 1 ½ tsp onion powder
- 1/2 tsp salt
- 1/2 tsp ground black pepper
- 4 cups boiling water

Directions:

1. Open the Instant Pot, and add all the ingredients. Seal and select "Manual" mode, adjusting the cooking time for 10 minutes on high pressure.
2. When the cooking time is over, press the "Cancel" button and opt for the quick pressure release.
3. After the pressure has been released, carefully open the Instant Pot and open the lid.
4. Mix the soup. Check the consistency and add some water or vegetable broth as needed and garnish with a pinch of black pepper powder.

Butternut Squash Apple & Ginger Soup

Ingredients

- 1 tsp olive oil
- 1 medium chopped onions
- 2 tsp minced fresh ginger
- 2 minced garlic cloves
- 14oz chopped butternut squash
- 2 chopped granny apples
- 2 chopped carrots

- 1 tsp ground cinnamon
- ½ tsp ground cumin
- 1/4 tsp coriander powder
- 5 cups vegetable broth
- salt
- pepper

Directions:

1. Switch on the Instant Pot and select "Sauté" mode. Add the olive oil and onion to the pot, and cook stirring until soft and browned, for about 4-5 minutes. Add in the minced garlic and ginger and stir for another minute.

2. Press "Cancel" and add the remaining ingredients. Just leave the apples aside.

3. Season with salt and pepper and stir all the ingredients.

4. Close and seal the Instant Pot, select "Manual" mode and cook at high pressure for 10 minutes. After the soup is ready, release the pressure naturally.

5. Open the Instant Pot and give the soup another stir.

6. Use a hand blender to blend the soup to puree. Check the consistency and add the seasoning if needed, and garnish with diced granny apples.

Carrot Apple Ginger Soup

Ingredients:

- 10 oz chopped carrots
- 1 large chopped onion
- 6 minced garlic cloves
- 2 tsp fresh ginger
- 3 medium sized chopped apples
- 2 tsp fresh thyme

- 2 tsp orange zest
- salt
- pepper
- 7 cups vegetable broth
- fresh thyme
- ½ tsp sage leaves

Directions:

1. Add all the ingredients to the Instant Pot and close the lid.

2. Press the "Manual" button, and adjust the cooking time to 14minutes.

3. When ready, open the valve to release the pressure quicker.

4. Once all the pressure is released, open the lid.

5. Stir all ingredients and insert a hand blender to blend all the ingredients to a smooth mixture. Enjoy the hot soup and garnish it with sage leaves.

Coconut Curry Lentil Soup

Ingredients

- 2 tsp olive oil
- 1 cup diced onions
- 1 tsp minced ginger
- 1 tsp curry powder
- 2 cups diced carrot
- 5 cups vegetable broth
- 3/4 cup red lentils

- 1 tsp Salt
- 1/4 tsp pepper powder
- Chopped cilantro
- ½ cup coconut milk
- 1 tsp smoked Paprika
- ½ tsp Cayenne pepper

Directions:

1. Open the Instant Pot and select "Sauté" option and then add olive oil and onion and stir to cook for 5 minutes

2. Add the ginger and curry powder and cook, stirring, for around 30 seconds. Add the carrots, vegetable broth, lentils, 1 teaspoon salt, and 1/4 teaspoon pepper. Mix well.

3. Close the lid of the Instant Pot. Press the "Manual" button and set the timer to 10 minutes. The Instant Pot then will start cooking. After the cooking time is up, opt for the quick pressure release.

4. Open the Instant Pot lid. Let the soup cool for a few minutes, then puree by inserting a hand blender directly into the pot. Adjust the seasoning by adding more salt and pepper if needed and then serve hot and enjoy!

Noodle Soup

Ingredients:

- 4 cups boiling water
- 4 ounces rice noodles
- ½ tsp garlic powder
- 1 tsp Coconut Powder
- 1/4 tsp ground ginger
- ⅛ tsp onion powder
- 1 teaspoon salt

Directions:

1. Switch on the Instant Pot and pour the boiling water.

2. Add the remaining ingredients to the pot and select "Soup" mode. Adjust the cooking time to 7 minutes on high pressure.

3. Once done, allow the pressure to be released naturally, and then open the Pot, pour the soup in your serving bowls and enjoy!

Indo Sweet Corn Soup

Ingredients:

- 6 cups vegetable broth
- 3 cups sweet corn kernels
- 1 ½ cup chopped and minced carrots
- 1 cup chopped and minced cabbage
- 1 tsp soy sauce

- 1 tsp sesame oil
- 2 tsp minced ginger
- 3 tsp minced garlic
- 1 tsp cumin powder
- A pinch of pepper powder

Directions:

1. Switch on the Instant Pot and add the vegetable broth, corn, carrot, cabbage, soy sauce, sesame oil, ginger, garlic, and cumin powder. Close and seal the pot.
2. Press the "Soup" button and adjust the cooking time to 10 minutes on high pressure.
3. Allow the pressure to be released naturally, once the cooking time is over.
4. Take a hand blender and blend about 3 cups of the soup to thicken and add back to the soup. Garnish it with pepper and enjoy the hot soup!

Lentil Spinach Soup

Ingredients:

- 1 cup soaked green lentils
- 1 chopped onion
- 1 tsp olive oil
- 6 crushed clove cloves
- 1 cup chopped and minced carrots
- 1 cup chopped and minced bell pepper
- ½ cup chopped spinach

- 3 tsp tomato paste
- 1 cup chopped cherry tomatoes
- 1 tsp cumin powder
- 1 tsp coriander powder
- 1 tsp turmeric powder
- 1 tsp salt
- 6 cups water

Directions:

1. Switch on the Instant Pot and select "Sauté" mode. Add the oil and allow it to heat, then add the onion and garlic and cook for 3 minutes.

2. Add the carrots, sweet peppers, spinach, and all the spices. Sauté for 5 more minute then add tomato paste and chopped cherry tomatoes, soaked lentils, and water. Mix well.

3. Close the lid of the Instant Pot and cancel the "Sauté" mode. Select "Manual" mode and cook on high pressure for 12 minutes.

4. Once the time is over, release the pressure, let the soup cool down for a few minutes. Serve and enjoy!

Creamy Tomato Vegan Soup

Ingredients

- 3 cups chopped carrots
- 1 cup chopped onion
- 2 stalks chopped celery
- 1 tsp chopped & minced garlic
- 5 large roasted and chopped tomatoes
- 1 tbsp olive oil

- 4 tbsp tomato paste
- 1 tsp dried basil
- 3 1/2 cups vegetable broth
- 1/2 tsp dried thyme
- 1 tsp salt
- ½ tsp Pepper powder

Directions:

1. Switch on the Instant Pot and select "Sauté" function, heat the olive oil. Then add in the carrots, onion, celery, and salt. Cook for 1-2 minutes, until the onions are translucent.
2. Add the garlic and continue to cook for about 1 more minute. Then add thyme, basil, pepper, and tomato paste and stir well.
3. Add in the tomatoes and vegetable broth, set the Instant Pot to high manual pressure for 15 minutes.
4. Once done, opt for the quick pressure release. Puree the soup, using a hand blender.
5. Serve hot and enjoy the creamy soup.

Green Vegetables & Bean Soup

Ingredients

- 1 cup chopped onions
- 1 chopped red bell pepper
- 1 chopped green bell pepper
- 1 chopped tomato
- 3 stalks chopped celery
- 1 cup black beans
- 1 tsp salt

- 1/2 tsp white pepper powder
- 1 tsp hot sauce
- 2 tsp chili powder
- 2 tsp cumin powder
- 1 bay leaves
- 7 cups vegetable broth

Directions:

1. Open the Instant Pot and add all the ingredients, then close and seal the vent.

2. Cook the soup on Manual mode adjusting it to high pressure for 40 minutes, and then let the pressure get released naturally.

3. Once done, remove the bay leaf.

4. Mix well and squeeze a lime to the soup, give one last mix and serve hot. You can serve with tortilla chips, or avocado for the best taste.

Kale & Potato Soup

Ingredients

- 2 tsp olive oil
- 1 ½ cups leeks
- 10-15 stems of Kale leaves chopped finely
- 8 cups salted vegetable broth
- 1 large diced potato
- 2 minced garlic cloves
- 1/2 tsp apple cider vinegar
- ½ pepper powder
- Chopped green onions for garnishing.

Directions:

1. Switch on the Instant Pot and add the oil and leeks and sauté slightly, using the "Sauté" mode, then add the vegetable broth, potatoes, and garlic and lock the lid.
2. Press "Cancel" and then select the "Manual" mode and set the timer to 8 minutes on high pressure.
3. Opt for the quick pressure release once the cooking time is up.
4. The potatoes will turn soft and mushy. Just mash them with a potato masher nicely. Now add the chopped kale, and lock the lid again. Set the timer to 2 minutes on high pressure. Release the pressure quickly, after the time is over.
5. Now add in the apple cider vinegar and season to taste with salt and pepper and serve hot!

Sweet Potato Lentil Soup

Ingredients

- 2 tbsp olive oil
- 2 chopped onions
- 4 cloves garlic, minced
- 1 chopped fennel bulb
- 2 tsp cumin powder
- 1 1/2 tsp coriander powder
- 1 1/2 cups diced carrots
- 2 1/2 cups chopped sweet potatoes

- 1 cup red lentils
- 3 large tomatoes crushed
- 6 cups vegetable broth
- 1 tsp salt
- 1/2 tsp pepper powder
- 2 tbsp brown sugar
- 1/2 cup chopped parsley

Directions:

1. Open your Instant Pot and select "Sauté" mode, add the oil and heat it for a minute, now add the onions, chopped fennel bulb and stir for about 2 minutes.
2. Now add the minced garlic, cumin powder, and coriander powder and cook for another minute. Then add chopped carrots, sweet potato, and red lentils. Mix well to combine. Add the crushed tomatoes and vegetable broth and stir well.
3. Cover the Instant Pot and seal the valve. Set it on the "Soup" mode and adjust the cooking time to 10 minutes on high pressure.
4. Once done, allow it to naturally release the pressure for about 10 minutes. Once the pressure is released, turn off the Instant Pot and remove the lid.
5. Now add 1 tsp salt, ½ tsp pepper, 2 tbsp of brown sugar and the ½ cup chopped parsley. Stir well to combine. Allow to cool down for a while and serve hot.

Carrot Curried Red Lentil Soup

Ingredients

- 2 tbsp olive oil
- 1/2 chopped onions
- 1 tsp chopped ginger
- 1 tbsp curry powder
- 2 diced carrots
- 5 cups vegetable broth

- 3/4 cup dried red lentils
- 1 tsp salt
- 1/2 tsp pepper powder
- fresh cilantro
- 1 cup coconut milk
- A dash cayenne pepper

Directions:

1. Open the Instant Pot and set it on "Sauté" mode, and then add the oil and allow it heat. Add onions and sauté it for a minute or until translucency. Now add the minced ginger and curry powder, stir well and cook for about 30 seconds.

2. Now add the carrots, vegetable broth, lentils, 1 tsp salt, and 1/4 teaspoon pepper. Stir to combine.

3. Close the lid and set the release valve to the sealing position. Press the "Manual" button and set the timer to 10 minutes. After the time is up, opt for the quick pressure release.

4. Uncover and let the soup cool for a few minutes, then puree by inserting a hand blender.

5. Taste and add salt and pepper if desired. Ladle into bowls, garnish if desired, and serve.

CHAPTER 3: ENERGIZING INSTANT POT BREAKFASTS

Brown Rice Casserole

Ingredients

- 2 cups uncooked brown rice

- 1 1/2 cup dried beans

- 6 cups water

- 3 large crushed tomatoes

- 1 tsp minced garlic

- 2 tsp onion powder

- 1 tsp chili powder

- 1 tsp salt

Directions:

1. Open your Instant Pot and add all the ingredients.
2. Close the lid and set the "Manual mode", adjusting the cooking time for 20 minutes on high pressure.
3. Once done, allow the pressure to be released naturally and then enjoy the meal!

Potato Hash

Ingredients

- 1 large diced potato
- 1 large diced sweet potato
- 2 chopped bell peppes
- 1 clove minced garlic
- 2 tbsp olive oil
- 1/2 tsp salt

- 1/2 tsp black pepper
- 1 tsp cumin powder
- 1 tsp paprika
- 1 pinch cayenne
- 1/2 cup water

Directions:

1.	Toss in a tbsp of olive oil and add all the vegetables and the spices. Mix well to combine

2.	Add the mix to your Instant Pot along with 1/2 cup water. Set it to "Manual" mode and adjust the cooking time to 10 minutes on high pressure.

3.	Allow for the pressure to be released naturally, and open the pot when the steam has evaporated. Select "Sauté". Cook for 5-6 minutes or until the potatoes start to brown.

4.	Divide between the plates and enjoy the potato hash.

Instant Pot Potato Salad

Ingredients

- 4 cups diced Idaho potatoes
- 1 ½ cups water
- 1 1/2 cups diced carrots
- 1 cup green peas
- 1 cup corn kernels

- 1/4 cup vegan mayonnaise
- 10 minced green olives
- 1 tsp black salt
- 1/2 tsp pepper powder

Directions:

1. Add the potatoes, water, and carrots into the Instant Pot, close it and set to "manual" mode on high pressure, for 10 minutes.
2. Manually release the pressure and open the lid. Add the peas and corn, and then close the lid again and cook on manual, low pressure, for one minute. Release the pressure manually.
3. Strain the vegetables and keep them aside.
4. Take a small bowl, add all the dressing ingredients and mix well.
5. In a large mixing bowl, add the vegetables and pour the dressing and mix to combine well.
6. You can serve the salad warm as it is or chill for an hour and serve cool.

Carrot Cake Oatmeal

Ingredients

- 1 cup steel-cut oats
- 2 cups water
- 1 cup milk
- 1 cup grated carrot
- 1/4 cup golden raisins
- 2 tsp maple syrup

- 1 1/2 tsp cinnamon powder
- 1/2 tsp nutmeg powder
- 1 1/4 tsp vanilla extract
- ¼ tsp salt
- 1/2 cup nuts - almonds, walnuts

Directions:

1. Add the steel-cut oats, water, milk, grated carrot, golden raisins, maple syrup, cinnamon powder, nutmeg powder, vanilla, and salt to the Instant Pot.

2. Stir gently to combine. Close the lid of the pot and set it to Manual mode on high pressure for 10 minutes.

3. When the cooking time is up, turn off your Instant Pot and allow the pressure to come down naturally. Now adjust the sweetness to taste; it will thicken a bit as it cools down.

4. Divide the oatmeal between four bowls and garnish with chopped nuts.

Instant Pot Bread

Ingredients

- 3 1/4 cups all-purpose flour
- 1 1/2 teaspoons salt
- 1 teaspoon yeast (quick-rise)
- 1 teaspoon granulated sugar

Directions:

1. Open the Instant Pot and insert a sheet of parchment paper into the bowl. Spray the parchment with oil.

2. Now add 3 1/4 cups flour with salt, yeast, and sugar in a large bowl. Add 1 1/2 cups warm water and keep mixing until the dough no longer sticks to the side of the bowl.

3. Now, take the prepared dough and add it into the pot. Close the lid and select the Yogurt setting. Set the time for 4 1/2 hrs.

4. Spread 1 tbsp of flour on the kitchen counter. Take out the dough together with the parchment. Remove the parchment and flip the dough onto the flour. The dough will be very soft. Fold the top edge over itself to the centre of the dough. Repeat around the edges, going clockwise, until you form a round loaf. Flip the loaf over and transfer to the same parchment, seam-side down.

5. Return to the Instant Pot bowl insert. Close lid and press Yogurt setting for 30 min.

6. Remove the dough from the Instant Pot once the cooking time is up and cover the top of the dough with a piece of foil. Introduce into the oven, preheated to 450 degrees F and bake in centre of the oven for 30 minutes.

7. Remove the foil and continue baking until the top of the loaf is golden-brown and cracked, for approximately 15 to 20 more minutes. Remove the bread to a rack to cool for 30 minutes before cutting and serving.

Three-minute Oats

Ingredients

- 2 cups water
- 1 cup almond milk
- 1 cup steel-cut oats
- 1/4 cup raisins
- cinnamon (to taste)
- non-stick cooking spray

Directions:

1. Switch on the Instant Pot and add the water, milk, oats, and raisins. Lock on the lid. Use the "Manual" function to cook for 3 minutes on high pressure.
2. When the time is up, let the pressure evaporate and open the pot. Carefully remove the lid, Check to see if the oats are cooked enough. If not, lock the lid and let the oats rest for 5-10 minutes without heating or cooking.
3. Then remove the lid. Stir and add the cinnamon. Serve hot with fresh fruits

Chili Lentils

Ingredients

- 1 large chopped onion
- 1 large chopped red bell pepper
- 7 cups vegetable broth
- 5 cloves finely chopped garlic
- 4 ½ tsp chili powder
- 1 package (15 oz) dry lentils
- 2 cans diced tomatoes
- 1/4 cup chopped fresh cilantro

Directions

1. Preheat your Instant Pot using the Sauté function. When hot, add the onion, bell pepper and sauté until vegetables are brown and begin to stick to the bottom of the pot, around 6 minutes.

2. Add in 3 tbsp of broth and continue to cook, stirring until the onions get soft and lightly browned. Stir in garlic and chili powder.

3. Cook 1 minute, mixing constantly. Add the lentils, tomatoes and remaining broth. Set the pot to Manual mode on high pressure for 15 minutes.

4. When done, let the pot release the pressure naturally, this would take about 10 minutes. Add cilantro and salt to taste. Enjoy!

Paleo Porridge

Ingredients

- ½ cup shredded coconut
- ¼ cup almond meal
- 1 tbsp flax seeds
- 1 tbsp chia seeds
- 1 tsp cinnamon powder
- 2 cups coconut milk

Directions:

1. Open the Instant Pot; combine all the ingredients in the pot.
2. Close the pot and seal the valve. Select Manual mode, adjusting the cooking time to 5 minutes on high pressure.
3. When done, opt for the natural pressure release. Transfer to your serving bowls and sprinkle the cinnamon on top.
4. Serve & Enjoy.

Instant Pot Pasta

Ingredients

- 10oz Pasta of your choice
- 6 cups water
- 1 cup of tomato basil sauce
- 1 broccoli head diced

Directions:

1. Add the pasta, 6 cups of water, diced broccoli and one cup of tomato basil sauce in your Instant Pot.
2. Close the lid and lock it so that the vent is sealed.
3. Press the Manual button and adjust the cooking time to 5 minutes on high pressure.
4. When the cooking time is over, allow the Instant Pot to release the pressure automatically.
5. Once the pressure is released, open the lid, and mix the pasta to combine well in the sauce.
6. In case the sauce is not thick enough, simmer it until it thickens using the Sauté function.
7. Serve and Enjoy.

Berry Jam

Ingredients

- 2 cups minced strawberries
- 1 cup blueberries
- 1 chopped apple
- 1/4 cup maple syrup
- 1/4 cup orange juice

Directions:

1. Wash the berries and mince the strawberries.
2. Switch on the Instant Pot and add all the ingredients. Cover and set to cook on Manual adjusting it to high pressure for 3 minutes.
3. After the cooking time is over, allow the pot to naturally release its pressure, this would take about 10 minutes.
4. Mash the mixture to your desired texture. Set the Instant Pot to Sauté mode and simmer the jam to thicken, mixing it regularly for about 10 minutes.
5. When it starts sticking to the bottom of the pot, it's almost ready.
6. The jam will continue to thicken while cooling. Store in the refrigerator in jars and it is ready to enjoy.

Instant Pot Oatmeal

Ingredients:

- 1 cup oats
- 2 cups water
- 1/2 cup almonds

- 1 cinnamon stick
- 1 pinch of salt

Directions:

1. Switch on the Instant Pot and add the oatmeal and water in the ratio indicated on the package, cinnamon stick, and a pinch of salt.
2. Press the Manual setting and set the cooking time for 3 minutes on high pressure. Once the cooking time ends, allow the oatmeal to rest in the pot during the natural release of the pressurized steam that takes 20 minutes.
3. Add the toppings (I love adding nuts) of your choice with some additional almond milk to your taste.

Rosemary Roasted Crispy Potatoes

Ingredients

- 13 red potatoes
- 1 cup water
- 2 tsp avocado oil

- 1 tbsp minced rosemary
- salt
- pepper

Directions:

1. Cut the potatoes into halves.
2. Add the water to your Instant Pot, place the potatoes into the steamer basket and cook at high pressure for 5 minutes. Wait 10-15 minutes to have all the remaining pressure released.
3. Remove the potatoes. Pat-dry your Instant Pot and pour some oil to the bottom. Select Sauté mode. Add the boiled and diced potatoes.
4. Sprinkle the rosemary over the potatoes. Allow the potatoes to brown or turn crispy for about 4 - 5 minutes.
5. Serve the potatoes sprinkled with salt and pepper.

Apple Spice Oats

Ingredients

- 1/2 cup steel-cut oats
- 1 chopped apple
- 1 1/2 cups water

- 1 tsp cinnamon powder
- 1/4 tsp allspice
- 1/8 tsp nutmeg

Directions:

1. Add the oats, apple, water, and spices to your Instant Pot. Close the lid and make sure the vent is closed. Select the manual setting and set to cook on high pressure for 4 minutes.
2. Allow the pressure to release naturally. This will take about 15 minutes. Open and add any sweetener of your choice (I usually add maple syrup) and serve.

Coconut creamy oats

Ingredients

- 1/2 cup coconut flakes
- 1 cup steel-cut oats
- 1 cup coconut milk
- 2 cups water

- 1 pinch salt
- 2 tablespoons brown sugar
- 1 cinnamon stick

Directions:

1. Add the dry coconut flakes to your Instant Pot and select Sauté function. Stir and watch closely to avoid burning.
2. When the coconut flakes begin to lightly brown, remove a half aside for the topping, and add the steel-cut oats to toast as well. Cook the oats and coconut flakes for a few more minutes, until both are fragrant.
3. Then add ½ of coconut milk and the rest of the ingredients. Stir to combine. Now, cancel sauté and select Manual mode adjusting the cooking time to 2 minutes on high pressure.
4. When the cooking time is complete, allow the pressure to be released naturally for 10 minutes.
5. Serve warm, topped with a drizzle of coconut milk, a spoonful of toasted coconut flakes.

Yogurt with Fruits

Ingredients

- 1 bottle (33.81 fl oz) soy milk
- 1 probiotic capsule
- 7 fruit spread

Directions:

1. Shake the soy milk can so that there are no solid remains at the bottom of the bottle or can. Open the probiotic capsule and add the powder to the soy milk.

2. Close the bottle and shake vigorously to mix the probiotic powder into the soy milk. Let it rest for a minute or two to allow the probiotic powder to dissolve.

3. You can select some shot glasses or small jars. Spread 1 tsp of fruit spread at the bottom of each glass. Now shake the soy milk one more time to be sure the probiotic powder is fully dissolved and evenly distributed in the soy milk.

4. Pour the soy milk mixture into the jars or glasses, on top of the fruit spread. DO NOT MIX the fruit spread and the soy milk mixture together, or the yogurt will not set up properly. Just leave the fruit on the bottom and the soy milk on top after the yogurt has set up.

5. Place the filled jars directly to the bottom of the stainless steel pot inside the Instant Pot. Move the jars together to stack more jars on top, if needed.

6. Plug in the Instant Pot and close the lid. Set the valve to vent. Adjust the time to 12 - 15 hours on Yogurt mode. The Instant Pot should start automatically after 10 seconds.

7. Carefully open the Instant Pot lid, remove the jars from the Instant Pot and allow them to cool on the counter for about 30-60 minutes before adding the lids and putting them into the refrigerator. Let the jars chill covered in the refrigerator for at least 2 hours.

8. When ready to serve, uncover the jars and gently pour off any liquid that may have collected on top of the yogurt.

9. Top with additional fresh fruits and berries, and nuts as desired

Buckwheat Porridge

Ingredients

- 1 ½ cup raw buckwheat
- 3 ½ cups rice milk
- 1 sliced banana
- 1/4 cup raisins

- 1 tsp cinnamon powder
- 1/2 tsp vanilla
- chopped nuts

Directions:

1. Wash and rinse the buckwheat and add it to the Instant Pot. Then add the rice milk, banana, raisins, cinnamon, and vanilla and close lid.

2. Select the Manual mode and set the cooking time to 6 minutes on high pressure. When the timer beeps at the end of the cooking cycle, turn the pot off and opt for the natural release of the pressure

3. Once the pressure is released, carefully open the lid and mix the porridge. Add more rice milk if necessary according to the needed consistency. Garnish with chopped nuts.

Blueberry Jam

Ingredients

- 1 pound blueberries
- 1/2 pound sugar
- 1 lemon

Directions:

1. Add the blueberries to a food processer or use a hand blender and puree them. Add the sugar and mix well. Refrigerate overnight to allow the flavors to blend. Add the lemon zest. Stir and mix well and add the mixture to the Instant Pot.

2. Click on Sauté mode and bring to a boil stirring often. Boil for 5 minutes. After 5 minutes, place lid on the pot, cancel the Sauté mode and opt for Manual mode, setting it to 10 minutes on high pressure.

3. Opt for the natural pressure release. Once the pressure is released naturally, remove the lid and set back to Sauté mode. Repeat the above step, by clicking on Sauté mode and allowing it boil for 5 minutes.

4. After that, pour into the jars and let the jam cool on the counter, then refrigerate it. The jam is ready to use.

Instant Pot Sago Stew

Ingredients

- 1 1/2 cups soaked sago
- 1 chopped green chili
- 2 small diced potatoes
- 2 grated carrots
- 1/2 cup green peas
- ½ tsp cumin seed
- 1 tsp lemon juice

- 1 tsp salt
- 1/2 tsp sugar
- 2 tsp oil
- 1/2 cup roasted and coarsely ground peanuts
- cilantro (for garnishing)

Directions:

1. Soak the sago in water overnight or for at least 5 hours. If there is any water left, drain it.
2. Add some oil to the Instant Pot and select Sauté mode. Add the cumin seeds and green chilies.
3. Toast them for 5 minutes, and then add the potatoes and salt. Cook the potatoes until they turn brown which may take 5minutes.
4. Then add the carrots and green peas and cook for another 2 minutes. Add the sago, peanut powder and sugar to the Instant Pot. Stir and mix well.
5. Change the setting to Manual mode, adjusting the cooking time to 10 minutes.
6. When the sago is cooked it should be transparent and not sticky. Mix the juice of one lemon and garnish with cilantro. Serve hot for breakfast or lunch.

Quinoa Breakfast Bowl

Ingredients

- 1/2 cup quinoa
- 1/4 cup mango chunks
- 1 tsp hemp seeds
- 1 tsp cacao nibs
- 2 cups almond milk

Directions:

1. Open the Instant Pot and add all the ingredients to the pot. Select Manual mode, setting the time to 10 minutes on high pressure.
2. Once done, allow the pressure to be released naturally. Mix everything well and serve hot for breakfast.

Peanuts Porridge

Ingredients

- 1 cup oatmeal
- 1 cup peanuts
- 1/2 tsp salt
- 1 tsp flour
- ½ tsp fresh nutmeg powder

- 1 tsp cornmeal
- 1/2 teaspoon vanilla extract
- 3/4 cup coconut milk
- 4 cups water

Directions

1. Take a blender and grind the oatmeal into a fine powder. Also, grind the peanuts until they are almost a smooth peanut butter.

2. Switch on the Instant pot, bring 1 cup of water to a boil, using the Sauté mode.

3. While the water is heating, mix together the flour, powdered oatmeal, peanuts, nutmeg powder, and cornmeal, pour in 1/2 cup of water, and keep stirring in more water until a loose, liquid paste is formed, which will take about 1 cup of water or so.

4. This paste should be wet enough to be poured into the boiling water. Keep stirring until no lumps remain. Cancel the Sauté function and select Manual mode, setting the time to 8 minutes on low pressure.

5. Remove the lid and add the vanilla and the coconut milk. Close the lid. Select the manual mode for about 10 more minutes. Once the pressure is released, serve hot.

CHAPTER 4: RICE, BEANS & LENTIL INSTANT POT RECIPES

Rosemary Lentils & Beans

Ingredients

- 4 cups water

- 1 1/2 cups brown rice

- 1 cup brown lentils

- 1 cup soaked navy beans

- 1 cup yams

- 1 tsp rosemary

- 1 tsp thyme

- 1 tsp minced garlic

- 1/2 cup chopped yellow onion

- 2 tbsp vegetable broth

- 1 lime

- vegan parmesan cheese for garnishing

- Arugula

Directions

1. Switch on the Instant pot, and select the Sauté mode. Heat the broth and sauté the onion for about 4 minutes until translucent, then add the garlic.

2. Add the rest of the ingredients to the pot and stir well. Close the lid and opt for Manual mod, setting the time to 25 minutes on high pressure.

3. Release the pressure naturally. Serve and garnish with lime and vegan cheese for a yummy flavor.

Jasmine Rice

Ingredients

- 1 cup white jasmine rice
- 2 cups water
- 1 teaspoon salt
- 1 teaspoon oil

Directions:

1. Start the Instant Pot and add the water, oil, salt, and rice. Close the lid, securing the vent in the sealing position.
2. Select the pressure cooker mode at high pressure for 5 minutes.
3. When the coking cycle is over, release the pressure and open the lid, Jasmine Rice is ready.

Chickpeas with Brown Rice

Ingredients

- 2 cups water

- 2 tsp curry paste

- 1/2 tsp salt

- 1 1/2 cups soaked brown basmati rice

- 1 cup soaked chickpeas

- ¼ cup toasted peanuts

- 2 tbsp diced green onions

- 1 avocado

- Cilantro, diced

- 1 tbsp hot sauce

- ½ red onion, diced

Directions:

1. Take 2 containers, fitting in the Intant Pot's steamer basket.
2. Pour two cups of water into the first container, the one you're going to use for rice. Add in the curry paste, and the salt. Add the rice.
3. Place the chickpeas in the second container.
4. Arrange the steamer rack in the Instant Pot, add 2 cups of water. Put the chickpea container, and stack the rice container.
5. Close the pot, and set it on manual cooking mode for about 22 minutes. Let the pressure naturally release when the cooking time is over.
6. Serve the brown rice with some chickpeas, and top with avocado slices, peanuts, herbs, and scallions and enjoy the floured rice.

Lentil Brown Rice

Ingredients

- 1 tbsp olive oil
- 1 large minced onion
- 2 cloves of garlic, minced
- 1 cup brown rice
- 1 cup lentils

- 2 cups vegetable broth
- 1 pinch of cinnamon powder
- 1 tsp salt
- ½ tsp pepper powder
- 1 chopped spring green onion

Directions:

1. Switch on the Instant Pot and select the Sauté mode. Add olive oil, then add the minced onion and garlic and sauté them for about 5 minutes until they become translucent.

2. Add the rice, vegetable broth, salt, lentils, and pepper. Cover the pot and seal the vent. Cancel the Sauté mode and select Manual mode, setting the cooking time to 15 minutes on high pressure.

3. Opt for the natural pressure release when the cooking time is up. Open the pot after the pressure has been released. Add more salt and pepper if needed. Transfer to a serving bowl and garnish with spring onions.

Dal Tadka

Ingredients

- 1 cup yellow-skinned lentils
- 1 inch chopped and minced ginger
- 1/2 teaspoon turmeric
- Salt as needed
- 1 tsp sugar
- 1 tablespoon oil or ghee as per your taste.
- 1/2 tsp cumin seed
- 1/2 cup finely chopped onion
- 4 cloves minced garlic
- 1 green chili pepper

Directions:

1. Switch on the Instant Pot, choose Sauté mode and add the oil or ghee as per your taste. Add the onions and cook until they are translucent. Then add the turmeric and all other ingredients.
2. Cancel Sauté mode and select Manual mode, adjusting the cooking time to 15 minutes on high pressure.
3. Allow the pressure to release naturally which may take 10 minutes. Serve the lentils hot with rice.

Mexican Rice

Ingredients

- 2 cups soaked long-grain brown rice
- 2 tablespoons olive oil
- ½ chopped onion
- 3 minced garlic cloves
- ½ tsp cumin powder
- ¼ cup tomato sauce
- 2 cups vegetable broth
- ½ teaspoon salt

Directions:

1. Plug in your Instant Pot and press "Saute" mode to heat it. Add the oil, then the onion, garlic, cumin and cook for 2 minutes.
2. Stir in the rice and sauté for about 5 minutes. Add the tomato sauce and mix well. Add vegetable broth and salt.
3. Click on the cancel button. Cover the Instant Pot, and opt for the Manual cooking mode, setting it up to 25 minutes on high pressure.
4. Let the Instant Pot release the pressure naturally. Once the steam is released, open the Instant Pot and serve the rice!

Spanish Pot

Ingredients

- 1/2 cup chopped small onions
- 1/2 cup chopped red bell pepper
- 2 cups white rice
- 3 ½ cups vegetable broth
- 1/2 tsp chili powder
- 1/4 tsp cumin powder
- 1 cup salsa

Directions:

1. Switch on the Instant Pot, add the chopped onions and peppers, add some vegetable broth to cover the bottom of the pot to prevent sticking and choose Sauté mode to cook the veggies until soft.
2. Add the remaining spices to the pot and stir well.
3. Wash the rice well and add it to the pot and combine everything well.
4. Add 1 cup of your favorite Salsa to the center of the pot.
5. Close the lid; make sure to seal the vent. Select Manual mode and adjust the time to 15 minutes on high pressure.
6. Once done, opt for the natural pressure release. Then carefully open the lid
7. Serve and enjoy the rice!

Coconut Curry Rice

Ingredients

- 1 can full-fat coconut milk (10oz)
- 1/2 cup water
- 1 tsp salt

- 2 tsp curry powder
- 1 cup jasmine rice
- Coriander or cilantro for garnish

Directions

1. Add all the ingredients to the Instant Pot and mix to combine.
2. Secure the lid and set the Instant Pot to Manual mode on high pressure for 8 minutes
3. Let it naturally release the pressure for 10 minutes. Once done, the rice is ready to serve. Garnish with cilantro or coriander leaves and grated fresh coconut.

Beans & Rice

Ingredients

- 1 1/2 cups red kidney beans
- 1 1/2 cups brown rice
- 1 cup salsa
- 1/2 bunch chopped cilantro
- 3 cups vegetable broth
- 2 cups water

Directions

1. Open the Instant Pot and add the dried Beans and Rice.
2. Pour the Vegetable Broth and Water over the Rice and Beans, then mix everything well.
3. Next, add the Salsa and chopped Cilantro into the pot. Do not mix!
4. Close the Instant Pot; select the Manual Mode to cook on High Pressure for 25 Minutes.
5. One the cooking time is over let the Instant Pot release the pressure for additional 10 minutes. Finally, release all the remaining pressure, and serve the Beans and Rice warm.

Sushi Rice

Ingredients

- 2 cups Japanese sushi rice
- 2 cups water
- 1/4 cup white wine vinegar
- 1/4 cup seasoned rice wine vinegar
- 1 1/2 tsp salt
- 2 tsp sugar

Directions

1. Add the rice and water to your Instant Pot and select the Rice mode, adjusting it to low pressure for 12 minutes. Once the cooking time is up, allow pressure to be naturally released for about 10 minutes.
2. Meanwhile, in a small bowl, combine white wine vinegar, rice wine vinegar, salt, and sugar. Microwave for 1 minute, and then stir until the sugar is completely dissolved.
3. Transfer the rice to a glass dish. Then using a wooden spoon, gently add the vinegar mixture and mix well to combine and roll into rolls together with other sushi ingredients of your choice and enjoy!

Asian Broccoli Rice

Ingredients

- 2 cups rice
- 2 1/2 cups water
- 1/4 cup soy sauce
- 2 cups broccoli florets
- 2 large minced garlic cloves

Directions

1. Switch on the Instant Pot; add the rice, water, and soy sauce. Then add the garlic and stir to combine all the ingredients. Add the broccoli and do not mix.
2. Close the lid and Press the Rice button. The program will start automatically on the pre-programmed settings.
3. When you hear the cooking time is over, opt for the natural pressure release, which takes 10-15 minutes. The open the lid carefully.
4. Serve hot and enjoy the rice.

Vegan Burritos

Ingredients

- 3 tablespoons water
- 1 tsp olive oil
- 1 chopped red onion
- 1 chopped red bell pepper
- 3 minced garlic cloves
- ½ cup black beans
- 1 1/2 cups uncooked brown rice
- 1 1/2 cups corn
- 1 cup chopped kale
- ½ cup salsa
- 1 jalapeno chili
- 8 tbsp vegan sour cream

- 2 cups water
- 1 tsp cumin powder
- 2 tsp chili powder
- 1 tsp salt
- 8 flour tortillas (10-12 inches)
- 3 cups fresh lettuce
- 2 chopped avocadoes
- 2 chopped tomatoes
- green onions for garnishing
- ¼ cup vegan cheese

Directions

To make the burrito filling:

1. Open your Instant Pot and select the Sauté mode. Add the olive oil, onion, red pepper and garlic. Cook for 2-3 minutes and cancel the sauté function.
2. Now add all the remaining filling ingredients to the Instant Pot, give them a little mix, close the lid, turn the valve to seal and select the Manual mode setting it to 25 minutes on high pressure.
3. Let the pressure get released naturally (usually this takes about 10 minutes). Carefully remove the lid and stir. Taste, add more spices or salt if desired.

To assemble the burritos:

Take 2 tablespoons of filling and add them to the centre of each tortilla. Add the fresh lettuce, avocado and other ingredients as per your requirements and taste. Fold two sides and serve immediately.

Vegetable Rice

Ingredients

- 3 cups basmati rice
- 4 1/2 cups water
- 1 cup chopped green beans
- 2 chopped large carrots
- 1 cup chopped red onion
- 1 minced garlic clove
- 1/2 inch ginger
- Salt as per taste

- 1 1/2 tsp coriander powder.
- 1 tsp cumin
- 1/2 tsp red chili powder
- 2 clove
- 1/2 tsp black pepper powder
- 1/2 tsp cinnamon
- 1 tablespoon tomato paste
- 4 tablespoons cashew nuts paste

Directions

1. Switch on the Instant Pot and pour the oil to the inner pot. Select Sauté mode and add the ginger and garlic and stir for a minute. Add the onions and cook until they turn slight brown.
2. Now add all the spices listed above and continue to stir. Add the tomato paste, carrots, green beans and keep stirring thoroughly for 2 minutes. Then add the cashew paste and stir well.
3. Now, pour the rice and water and stir well to combine everything thoroughly. Cancel the Sauté mode.
4. Close the lid of the Instant Pot. Select the Manual mode and set it to 15 minutes on high pressure. When the cooking time is up, release the pressure naturally which may take around 10 minutes.
5. Garnish with fried cashew nuts and cilantro.

Cajun Vegetable Treat

Ingredients

- 1 tsp olive oil
- 1/2 diced onion
- 1 cup basmati rice
- 2 cups water
- 1/2 tsp chili powder
- 1/3 tsp dried thyme
- 1/3 tsp dried oregano
- 1/2 tsp smoked paprika

- 1/2 cumin powder
- 1 1/2 cups frozen vegetables
- 2 tablespoons tomato puree
- Salt as needed
- A pinch black pepper
- 1 lime
- fresh coriander

Directions

1. Set the Instant Pot to Sauté mode and add the olive oil followed by the diced onions. Cook until the onions turn translucent.
2. Stir in the rice and all the spices, mixing until very well combined. Add your choice of frozen vegetables, the water and the tomato puree.
3. Cancel sauté and close the lid, set the vent to Sealing position and select Manual mode. Set to 10 minutes on high pressure. Do a quick pressure release once the cooking cycle is over and season well with salt and a pinch of black pepper, a squeeze of lime juice and chopped fresh coriander. Serve hot!

Rice & Lentils

Ingredients

- 1 tsp oil
- 1/2 cup chopped onion
- 2 cloves minced garlic
- 3 1/2 cups water
- 1 1/2 cups brown rice
- 1 cup brown lentils

- 1 cup diced potatoes
- 2 tsp fresh rosemary
- 1 tsp fresh thyme
- salt
- Pepper

Directions

1. Switch on the pot, click on Sauté mode, heat the oil. Add the onion and sauté until browned for 5 minutes. Then add the garlic and sauté for another minute.

2. Now cancel the Sauté mode and click on Manual mode, add the water, brown rice, lentils, potatoes rosemary and thyme to the onion mixture and stir to combine.

3. Close the lid and make sure that the vent is sealed. Cook on high pressure for 25 minutes. Let the pressure get released naturally. Open the lid and season with salt and pepper. Garnish with fresh thyme and rosemary.

Rice & black-eyed Peas Curry

Ingredients

- 1 cup diced onions
- 4 cloves minced garlic
- 2 cups brown rice
- 2 cups black beans

- 6 cups water
- 1 teaspoon salt
- 1 lime squeezed
- 1 avocado sliced

Directions

1. Add the diced onion and garlic into the Instant Pot. Then add the brown rice and black beans.
2. Pour the water into the pot and add the salt.
3. Secure the lid with the vent sealed. Select Manual mode and cook for 30 minutes on high pressure.
4. Allow the pressure to get naturally released which may take 10 minutes.
5. Serve in bowls and squeeze a lime over the bowl and stir. Then add a few slices of avocado for garnishing.

Spiced Quinoa & Cauliflower Rice

Ingredients

- 1 tbsp olive oil
- 1 onion, chopped
- 1 cup quinoa
- 2 minced garlic cloves
- 1 inch grated fresh ginger
- 1 tsp ground turmeric
- 1 tsp cumin powder
- 1 tsp coriander powder
- 2 cups vegetable broth

- 1 (8oz) packet tofu cut into cubes
- 2 chopped bell peppers
- 1/4 cup cilantro leaves
- 1/4 cup toasted slivered almonds
- 4 tsp lemon juice
- salt
- Pepper

Directions

1. Select the Sauté mode and add the olive oil and sauté the onions until soft Add in the quinoa, garlic, ginger and stir for another minute or two to allow the quinoa to lightly toast.

2. Then add all the spices, including a pinch of salt and pepper, and fry until fragrant, for about 30 seconds. Add the vegetable broth.

3. Now, add in the tofu, bell pepper, and remaining broth into the pot. Stir in everything well and Press cancel to turn off the Sauté mode.

4. Seal the Instant Pot and select the Manual mode setting it to 10 minutes on high pressure. After the cooking time is up, opt for the natural pressure release. Last, add in the sliced almonds, fresh cilantro, lemon juice and give it a gentle stir.

5. The add salt and pepper if needed. Divide between the bowls and serve warm.

Vegan Pudding

Ingredients

- 1 1/2 cups coconut milk
- 1 cup water
- 3/4 cup brown basmati rice
- 1 teaspoon pure vanilla extract

- 2 teaspoons cinnamon
- 1/2 teaspoon nutmeg
- 1 pinch sea salt
- maple syrup (to taste)

Directions

1. Switch on the Instant Pot and add the coconut milk, water, rice, vanilla, cinnamon and salt to your Instant Pot.

2. Stir to combine. Close the lid. Select the Porridge mode and cook for 20 minutes.

3. Once done, allow the pressure to be released naturally which may take 10 minutes. Then open the lid, add the maple syrup and enjoy chilled!

Cilantro Peas Rice

Ingredients

- 1 cup soaked peas
- 2 cups basmati rice
- 4 1/2 cups water
- salt
- 1 tbsp olive oil
- 2 tsp cinnamon
- 1 bay leaf

- 3 green cardamom cloves
- 1/2 cup grated coconut
- 3/4 cup chopped cilantro
- 4 green chilies
- 1 garlic clove
- 1/4 inch ginger grated

Directions

1. Start by blending the coconut, garlic, cilantro leaves, green chilies, ginger and 1 cup water to a smooth paste consistency and place aside.
2. Add the oil to the Instant Pot. Press Sauté mode and as the oil heats up, add the cinnamon, green cardamom, and bay leaf. Stir continuously for 20 seconds, then add the soaked rice and peas and continue to stir for a minute.
3. Add the cilantro paste and mix evenly. Add the water and salt. Stir well.
4. Close the lid of the Instant Pot. Press Manual mode and set the time for 10 minutes on high pressure. Once done, release the pressure naturally which may take 5 minutes and garnish with fresh cilantro and serve.

Mushroom risotto

Ingredients

- 1/2 cup minced white onion
- 3 cloves garlic minced
- 1 tbsp olive oil
- 6-8 large mushrooms chopped
- 1 tsp salt
- 1 tsp thyme
- 1/2 cup dry white wine

- 3 cups vegetable broth
- 1 cup arborio rice
- 1/4 cup lemon juice
- 2 cups fresh spinach
- 1 tsp vegan butter
- 1 1/2 tsp nutritional yeast
- black pepper

Directions

1. Using the Sauté mode, add the oil, onions and garlic and sauté them for about 3 minutes.
2. Add the rice, mix well and add the vegetable broth, wine, salt, thyme and mushrooms. Close the lid and turn the vent to sealed position. Select the Manual mode and set the time to 10 minutes. Once done, use the quick pressure release and open the lid.
3. Add in the spinach, nutritional yeast, black pepper and vegan butter. Stir very well until you get the desired thick sauce and serve warm.

CHAPTER 5: MOUTHWATERING INSTANT POT DESSERTS

Apple Sauce

Ingredients

- 5 medium green apples
- 2 tsp sugar
- 1 tsp cinnamon
- ¼ cup water

Directions

1. Wash, peel and chop the apples and keep aside.
2. Now add the cinnamon and sugar to a large bowl and mix well. Add the cubed apples and thoroughly mix in the cinnamon and sugar. Pour the water on the chopped apples. And mix well again.
3. Add the apples to your Instant Pot, close and set the Instant Pot on Manual mode for 3 minutes.
4. Once done, release the pressure naturally and open the lid. Transfer the applesauce from the pot to a bowl, puree using a hand blender, or leave the chunks, if you prefer your sauce with chunks and allow cooling before serving.

Rice Dessert

Ingredients

- 2 cups sticky rice
- 1 cup water
- 1/3 cup brown sugar
- 1 tsp soy sauce
- 2 tsp sesame oil
- 1/2 cup jujube dates
- 1 tbsp pine nuts
- 2-3 tbsp chestnuts

Directions

1. Soak the sweet sticky rice in water for about 6 hours. Prepare jujube dates by washing them thoroughly and cutting them lengthwise.
2. Take the chestnuts and chop it in small pieces. Drain the sticky rice. Add the sesame oil to the Instant Pot to coat the bottom. Add the drained rice, soy sauce, sugar and water. Mix everything thoroughly.
3. Add the chestnuts, jujube dates and pine nuts. Close the lid and set the Instant Pot to Manual mode, adjusting the time to 8 minutes on Low Pressure.
4. Allow the pressure to be released naturally which may take 10-15 minutes.
5. Open the lid and mix the rice again, it will get darker in a few minutes.
6. Serve warm as it is or put it in a cupcake mold.

Baked Apples

Ingredients

- 8 apples
- 1/2 cup raisins
- 1 tablespoon cinnamon
- 1/3 cup water

Directions

1. Switch on the Instant Pot and add the water. Cut out holes on top of each apple. Put the apples in the Instant Pot and Sprinkle with cinnamon and stuff with raisins.
2. Close the Instant Pot and turn the valve to the Sealing position. Select the Manual mode from the menu and set the time to 5 minutes. When the cooking time is over allow the Instant Pot to release the pressure manually.
3. Carefully remove your baked apples from the Instant Pot and enjoy!

Sugar-free Caramel Sauce

Ingredients

- 1 cup coconut cream
- 3/4 cup pure maple syrup
- 1/4 cup refined coconut oil

- 1 tsp pure vanilla extract
- 1 pinch salt

Directions:

1. Open your Instant Pot and add the coconut cream, maple syrup, and coconut oil to the Pot, then select the Sauté mode.
2. Stir until the coconut oil and coconut cream start boiling. Allow to boil for 15 minutes, keep mixing occasionally, and then turn off the Instant Pot.
3. Add in the pure vanilla extract and pinch of salt. Let cool slightly and transfer to a container, and refrigerate before serving.

Vegan Rice Pudding

Ingredients

- 1 1/2 cups Almond milk
- 1/2 cup water
- 3/4 cup brown basmati rice
- 2 teaspoons cinnamon
- 1/2 teaspoon nutmeg
- 1 pinch salt
- maple syrup (to taste)
- Chopped nuts of your choice.

Directions

1. Add the almond milk, water, rice, cinnamon and salt into the Instant Pot. Mix well all the ingredients.
2. Close the lid. Turn on the porridge mode and cook for 20 minutes. Then cancel and release the pressure quickly before opening the lid carefully.
3. Add the maple syrup to taste. Sprinkle with your favorite nuts and enjoy!

Strawberry Jam

Ingredients

- 1 cup minced strawberries
- 1 large orange juice

- 1/2 cup sugar

Directions

1. Place the strawberries in the Instant Pot. Pour the sugar and the juice from the orange over the strawberries. Close the lid and secure the vent.
2. Select the manual mode and set the time to 10 minutes under low pressure.
3. When it beeps, turn off the Instant Pot and opt for the natural pressure release.
4. Open the lid, pour the mixture into a food processor, or use a hand blender to blend it coarsely. Then scoop into your jam jars.
5. Refrigerate it and serve with breads or ice-cream and enjoy!

Tapioca Pudding

Ingredients

- 1 cup water
- 1 cup full-fat coconut milk
- 1/3 cup tapioca pearls
- 3 tbsp cup maple syrup

- 1 tsp vanilla extract
- 1 pinch salt
- 1/4 tsp ground nutmeg

Directions

1. Switch on the Instant Pot, add the water to the pot and add the tapioca pearls. Select the sauté mode and boil the pearls, then simmer them for 15 minutes.
2. Then add the rest of the ingredients; close the pot and seal the valve. Now set the pot on manual mode for 5 minutes on low pressure.
3. Once done, allow the pressure to be released naturally which may take about 10 minutes. Then open the lid carefully and mix all the ingredients well.
4. Serve the pudding in bowls and garnish it with a pinch of nutmeg and nuts.

Oats and Coconut Milk Kheer

Ingredients

- 1/2 cup steel-cut oats
- 1/2 cup Jaggery
- 1 cup water
- 1 (10 oz) can coconut milk

- 2 tsp coconut oil
- 2 tbsp cashew nuts
- 1/4 tsp cardamom powder
- 2 tbsp grated coconut

Directions

1. Switch on the Instant Pot and add the water as mentioned and the oats and close the lid and cook the oats for 5 minutes on manual mode at low pressure. Opt for the quick pressure release. Allow the pressure to be released manually.
2. Meanwhile, in a heavy bottom pan, add the jaggery and water. Let it come to a boil and then strain the mixture to remove any impurities.
3. Mash the cooked oats and add the jaggery mixture to the oats and stir it well. Then add the coconut milk. Close the pot and cook on Manual mode under low pressure for another 5 minutes.
4. Heat the coconut oil in a small pan and roast the cashew nuts and the grated coconut. Add this along with cardamom powder to the Oats and mix well. Serve warm or at room temperature.

Red Bean Rice Cake

Ingredients

- 3 cups water
- 1 cup sugar
- 1 ½ sweet rice flour

- 1/2 cup oil
- 1/2 tsp vanilla
- 2 1/2 cups cooked adzuki beans

Directions:

1. Take a large bowl, and mix together the water and sugar until the sugar is dissolved.

2. Whisk in the rice flour until well-blended. Then keep adding in the oil gradually until combined. Add vanilla and adzuki beans. Stir to combine. Divide the batter between two plastic wrap-lined 6" round cake pans, or one 8" round pan

3. Place the steam trivet into the Instant Pot. Add 1 cup of water. Place the cake pan on the trivet. Cover and cook at high pressure for 30 minutes on Manual mode. Let the pressure to be released naturally. Serve and enjoy the cake!

Vegan Lemon Cheesecake

Ingredients

- 12 gingersnap cookies
- 1 1/2 tsp almonds (toasted)
- 1/2 tsp vegan margarine
- 2 cups vegan cream cheese
- 1/2 cup granulated sugar
- 4oz silken tofu

- 1 medium lemon
- 1 tsp fresh lemon juice
- 1/2 tsp lemon extract
- 1 tsp vanilla extract
- 2 cups water

Directions

1. Take a non-stick pan and grease it with some oil or cooking spray.

2. Add the cookies and almonds to a blender and pulse to get cookie crumbs .Then add the melted vegan margarine and blend it well.

3. Chop the nuts finely. Transfer the crumb mixture to the pan and press it down into the bottom.

4. Take the cream cheese and add it to the blender along with the sugar and blend until smooth. Then add the tofu, lemon zest, lemon juice, lemon extract, and vanilla. Blend for 10 seconds or until smooth.

5. Place the pan in the center of two 12-inch by 12-inch pieces of aluminum foil. Fix the foil to seal the bottom of the pan. Transfer the cheesecake batter into the pan. Pour the water into the Instant Pot and insert the steaming trivet.

6. Set the pan on the trivet. Close the lid and, select the Manual mode, and adjust the cooking time to 10 minutes on high pressure.

7. When done, let the pressure get released naturally, then unlock the lid. Remove the top foil. If any moisture has accumulated on top of the cheesecake, dab it with a piece of paper towel to remove it. Let cool to the room temperature and then remove the cake from the pan. Serve and enjoy!

Vegan Coconut Yogurt

Ingredients

- 2 cans full fat coconut milk
- 1 tsp agar

- 1 tsp maple syrup
- 1 tsp probiotic powder

Directions

1. In the bowl of your Instant Pot, combine the coconut milk and agar and bring the mixture to a boil by using the sauté mode.
2. Use a whisk to keep stirring the mixture. Ensure that the agar dissolves in the coconut milk
3. Once the milk has reached a rolling boil turn off the Instant Pot and then stir in the maple syrup. Let the mixture cool to 110-115°F for proper fermentation.
4. Once the coconut milk has cooled, add in the probiotic powder and mix well. Now, select the "Yogurt" mode, and then use the arrows to set the amount of time you'd like the yogurt to ferment, usually 8 hours are enough to achieve the best consistency. Close the Instant Pot to help keep the yogurt clean and at the proper temperature.
5. Once the cooking cycle is over, open the Instant Pot.
6. Pour the yogurt into a clean jar with a lid, and store it in the fridge to set. The yogurt will thicken when chilled.
7. The coconut milk yogurt may separate a bit when stored in the fridge, so stir it well before serving.

Poached Pears

Ingredients

- 4 Bartlett pears
- 3 cups water
- 1 ½ cup red wine
- 1 cup pure pomegranate juice
- ½ cup sugar
- 1 orange, juiced and zested
- 1 tsp balsamic vinegar
- 3 cinnamon sticks
- 1 tsp whole cloves
- ½ cup cup pistachios

Directions

1. Wash the pears, peel and scoop out the seeds and cut the base so the pears can stand.
2. Set Instant Pot on the sauté mode and add the water, red wine, pomegranate juice, sugar, orange juice, orange zest, balsamic vinegar, cinnamon sticks, and whole cloves and keep stirring the liquid mixture until it begins to slightly simmer.
3. Now, add the pears, cancel Sauté mode and select the Manual mode instead. Cover and lock the Instant Pot lid and set the time to 10 minutes on high pressure. Once done, allow the pressure to get released naturally. Remove the lid. Carefully remove the pears and let cool. Strain out the cinnamon sticks, cloves, and orange zest.
4. Divide the pears between the serving plates. Drizzle the wine sauce to coat the pears and pour some more in the plate. Sprinkle with chopped pistachios and serve!

Paleo Rosemary Applesauce

Ingredients

- 10- 14 apples
- 1 fresh rosemary
- 1/2 cup water
- 4 tsp maple sugar
- 2 tsp spice mix (apple pie, cinnamon, nutmeg, clove)

Directions

1. Chop the apples into cubes. Don't peel the skin.

2. Now, switch on the Instant pot, add the apple cubes, water, spice mix and select the Manual mode, setting it on high pressure for 5 minutes.

3. Once done, opt for natural pressure release, which takes another 10 minutes.

4. Open the lid carefully, insert a hand blender and puree the sauce lightly, add the rosemary and maple sugar and stir in thoroughly and enjoy the sauce.

Chai Rice Pudding

Ingredients

- 1 cup short grain rice
- 1 cup almond milk
- 1 cup coconut milk
- 1 cup water
- 2 tsp brown sugar
- 6 sliced Medjool dates
- 1 tsp cinnamon powder
- 1 tsp ground ginger powder
- ¼ tsp ground nutmeg
- 2 cardamom pods
- 1 tsp vanilla extract
- Pinch of salt
- Nuts and fruits for garnishing.

Directions

1. Open your Instant Pot; add all the above ingredients except the garnishing.
2. Set the Instant Pot and select the manual mode and cook on high pressure for about 10 minutes.
3. Once done, allow the pressure to release on its own which may take another 10 minutes. Open the lid, and then add almond milk, only if needed depending on the consistency and serve in bowls adding the nuts & fruits of your choice.

Orange Spice Cake

Ingredients

- **_DRY INGREDIENTS_**
    - 1¼ cups whole-wheat flour
    - 1½ tsp cinnamon powder
    - 1 tsp allspice powder
    - ½ tsp baking soda
    - ½ tsp baking powder
    - ¼ tsp ground cloves
- **_WET INGREDIENTS_**
    - ½ cup orange juice with pulp
    - 1/3 cup maple syrup
    - 2 tbsp coarse flaxseeds
    - 3 tbsp melted coconut oil
- **MIX-INS**
    - 2 tbsp orange zest
    - ¾ cup dried cranberries
    - ½ cup chopped walnuts

Directions

1. Oil a 7-8 inch pan with some cooking spray and keep aside.
2. Take the dry ingredients, add the flour, cinnamon, allspice, baking soda and cloves to a medium- size mixing bowl and mix them thoroughly.
3. Take a larger bowl for the wet ingredients and add the juice, syrup, flax seeds and oil, now add the dry ingredients to the wet ones and mix well.
4. Spread the cake mixture into your prepared pan and cover with foil.
5. Switch on the Instant Pot, pour in 1½ cups water and add the stainless steel steam rack. Place the pan carefully into the cooker. Close the lid, and make sure the steam release handle is set to sealing, and cook on high pressure for 35 minutes. Opt for the natural pressure release.
6. Once the pressure indicator goes down, remove the lid, lift out the pan and remove the foil covering the pan.
7. Once cool, serve it and enjoy!

Apple Cranberry Crisp

Ingredients

- 3 medium apples, chopped
- 2 pears cubed
- 1 1/2 cups cranberries
- 1 tsp lemon juice
- 1/2 cup maple syrup
- 2 tsp arrowroot powder
- 1/2 tsp ginger powder
- 1/4 tsp nutmeg
- 2 tsp cinnamon powder
- 1/2 tsp allspice
- 1/4 tsp clove
- 1 cardamom pod
- 1 tsp dried orange peel
- 1/2 cup coconut flour
- 1 tsp chia seeds
- 1 cup shredded dried coconut
- 1/2 cup walnuts
- 1 pinch nutmeg
- 1/4 teaspoon sea salt
- 1/2 cup coconut oil

Directions

For the Filling :

Take the cubed apples and pears and cranberry juice and lemon juice and mix well thoroughly.

To make the topping :

Take a small mixing bowl, combine the coconut flour, chia seeds, coconut, nuts, maple syrup, spices, and salt. Add the coconut oil and then mix gently with a fork until evenly distributed.

To make the apple cranberry Crisp

1. Layer the topping over the filling ingredients in a baking dish. Add 2 cups of water to the Instant Pot and place a steamer trivet inside. Insert the baking dish into the pot carefully and cover it with the aluminum foil.

2. Close the lid, set the Instant Pot on Manual mode to high pressure for 20 minutes. Then opt for the quick pressure release. Open the lid carefully and remove the crisp from the cooker.

3. NOTE - For a crispier, crunchier top, introduce the baking dish into the oven and bake for 5-8 minutes. Then serve with a dollop of whipped cream or ice cream. Enjoy!

Apple and Lavender Cake

Ingredients

- 2 cups water
- 4 small apples
- 2 tsp lemon juice
- ½ tsp dried lavender flowers
- 1 ½ cup gluten-free flour
- 2 tsp coconut flour
- ½ tsp baking powder
- Pinch salt
- ⅓ cup palm shortening, melted
- 3 tsp maple syrup
- 1 tsp vanilla extract
- 1 tsp gelatin powder

Directions

1. Add the water to the Instant Pot and insert the steaming basket.
2. Take a baking dish, which fits the steaming basket, and line the bottom of the pan with parchment paper.
3. In a dish, mix the apples, lemon juice, and lavender together. Neatly spread apples evenly over the bottom of the cake pan.
4. Take a large mixing bowl, add the gluten-free flour and coconut flour, baking powder, salt and combine well.
5. In a separate bowl, mix together the palm shortening, maple syrup, and vanilla extract and stir well.
6. Sprinkle the gelatin powder over the palm shortening mixture and whisk vigorously until well-blended.
7. Add the above mixture over the dry ingredients and mix well enough to form a dough. Transfer the dough on the parchment paper and spread to fit the cake tin size. Cover the apples with the dough evenly.
8. Cover the cake pan with aluminum foil, tucking it in all around the rim.
9. Place the cake pan on the steaming basket. Close and lock the lid. Select "Manual" mode and set the time to 25 minutes on high pressure.
10. When the time is up, let the pressure get released naturally.
11. To serve, turn the cake pan upside down and unmold on a serving platter. Serve with a scoop of ice-cream!

Blueberry Mug Cake

Ingredients

- 1/3 cup almond flour
- 1 egg
- 1 tablespoon maple syrup
- 1/2 teaspoon vanilla
- 1/8 teaspoon salt
- 1/2 cup blueberries

Directions

1. Combine all the ingredients in a small bowl.
2. Add the batter to 1-2 mason jars, making sure you do not fill them fully to avoid the spilling out during cooking.
3. Place a steamer trivet into the Instant Pot and add 1 cup of water.
4. Cover the jars with some foil and place on the trivet.
5. Select MANUAL mode and adjust the time to 10 minutes on high pressure.
6. Once the program is complete, quickly release the pressure.
7. Remove the jars using the tongs and place on a cooling rack. Enjoy warm or chilled

Chocolate Chip Raspberry Mug Cake

Ingredients

- 1/3 cup almond flour
- 1 egg
- 1 tablespoon maple syrup
- 1/2 teaspoon vanilla extract
- 1/8 teaspoon salt
- 1/2 cup raspberries
- 1-1/2 tablespoons chocolate chips

Directions

1. Combine all the ingredients in a small bowl.
2. Add the batter to 1-2 mason jars, making sure you do not fill them fully to avoid the spilling out during cooking.
3. Place a steamer trivet into the Instant Pot and add 1 cup of water.
4. Cover the jars with some foil and place on the trivet.
5. Select MANUAL mode and adjust the time to 10 minutes on high pressure.
6. Once the program is complete, quickly release the pressure.
7. Remove the jars using the tongs and place on a cooling rack. Enjoy warm or chilled

Apple Cinnamon Mug Cake

Ingredients

- 1/3 cup almond flour
- 1 egg
- 1 tablespoon maple syrup
- 1/2 teaspoon vanilla extract
- 1/8 teaspoon salt
- 1/2 cup apples, diced finely
- 1/4 teaspoon cinnamon

Directions

1. Combine all the ingredients in a small bowl.
2. Add the batter to 1-2 mason jars, making sure you do not fill them fully to avoid the spilling out during cooking.
3. Place a steamer trivet into the Instant Pot and add 1 cup of water.
4. Cover the jars with some foil and place on the trivet.
5. Select MANUAL mode and adjust the time to 10 minutes on high pressure.
6. Once the program is complete, quickly release the pressure.
7. Remove the jars using the tongs and place on a cooling rack. Enjoy warm or chilled

Banana Chocolate Mug Cake

Ingredients

- 1/3 cup almond flour
- 1 egg
- 1 tablespoon maple syrup
- 1/2 teaspoon vanilla
- 1/8 teaspoon salt
- 1/2 tablespoon cocoa powder
- 1/2 banana, diced

Directions

1. Combine all the ingredients in a small bowl.
2. Add the batter to 1-2 mason jars, making sure you do not fill them fully to avoid the spilling out during cooking.
3. Place a steamer trivet into the Instant Pot and add 1 cup of water.
4. Cover the jars with some foil and place on the trivet.
5. Select MANUAL mode and adjust the time to 10 minutes on high pressure.
6. Once the program is complete, quickly release the pressure.
7. Remove the jars using the tongs and place on a cooling rack. Enjoy warm or chilled

Almond Carrot Cake

Ingredients

- 3 eggs
- 1 cup almond flour
- 2/3 cup Swerve
- 1 tsp baking powder
- 1 ½ tsp apple pie spice
- 1/4 cup coconut oil
- 1/2 cup heavy whipping cream
- 1 cup grated carrots
- 1/2 cup walnuts chopped

Directions:

1. Coat a 6-inch cake pan with some cooking spray.

2. Take a large mixing bowl; add all the ingredients as per the measurements and insert a hand blender to mix everything thoroughly.

3. Now pour the dough into the greased pan and cover the pan with a piece of foil.

4. Switch on the Instant Pot, pour two cups of water, and place a steamer rack. Place the cake pan carefully on the rack.

5. Select the CAKE mode and allow it to cook for 40 minutes. Opt for the natural pressure release when the cooking time is over.

6. NOTE - If you don't have the cake mode, just set your Instant Pot to Manual mode, adjusting the time to 20 minutes on high pressure.

7. Let it cool before coating it with a frosting of your choice or top with some nuts and coconut flakes.

Almond Coconut Cake

Ingredients

Dry Ingredients

- 1 cup almond flour
- 1/2 cup unsweetened shredded coconut
- 1/3 cup Truvia sweetener
- 1 tsp baking powder
- 1 tsp apple pie spice

Wet ingredients

- 2 eggs lightly whisked
- 1/4 cup butter melted
- 1/2 cup heavy whipping cream

Directions

1. Take a small mixing bowl and add all the wet ingredients and mix thoroughly.

2. Now, take a large bowl, add the dry ingredients, mix well and start adding the wet ingredients slowly and keep stirring well. Or insert a hand blender and blend everything well till the dough looks soft and fluffy.

3. Now, take a greased pan of about 6 inches and pour the mixture inside, set it well, cover it with the foil, tuck some wholes around the pan, and seal the foil well.

4. Switch on the Instant Pot, add 2 cups of water, insert a steaming trivet, place the pan carefully inside the pot and close the lid.

5. Select Manual mode and set it on high pressure for about 40 minutes

6. Once done, allow the pressure to be released naturally, open the lid and remove the foil. Allow it cool, garnish with nuts and cream and serve.

Almond Cheesecake

Ingredients

- 2 tsp lemon juice
- 2 tsp almond extract
- 1/4 cup sour cream

- 1/2 cup Swerve baking blend
- 1 cup cream cheese
- 2 eggs

For topping

- 1/4 cup sour cream
- 2 teaspoons Swerve

Directions

1. Open your Instant Pot, pour in two cups of water, and place a trivet inside.
2. In a food processor, add all the ingredients except eggs and topping ingredients. Start mixing.
3. Add both eggs and at this point blend well to get pourable liquid batter.
4. Take a 6-inch pan. Pour the mixture into the pan. Cover the pan with a piece of foil and place the pan on the trivet.
5. Close the lid, set to Manual mode, adjusting it to high pressure for 20 minutes, and then let it release the pressure naturally.
6. Mix up the sour cream and swerve for the topping.
7. Take out the cheesecake and spread the topping all over it.
8. Put it in the fridge, and take out when ready to serve.

Walnut Dark Chocolate Cake

Ingredients

- 1 cup almond flour
- 2/3 cup Swerve
- 1/4 cup unsweetened cocoa powder
- 1/4 cup chopped walnuts
- 1 tsp baking powder
- 3 eggs
- 1/3 cup heavy whipping cream
- 1/4 cup coconut oil

Directions:

1. Take a mixing bowl, add all the ingredients and insert a hand blender to mix everything well until the dough looks soft and fluffy.

2. Grease a pan that fits into the Instant Pot with some cooking spray. Pour the cake batter into this pan.

3. Insert a steaming rack into the Instant Pot and pour 1-2 cups of water inside. Place the cake pan on the rack.

4. Close the Instant Pot, and set it to Manual mode, adjusting the cooking time to 20 minutes under high pressure.

5. Opt for the natural pressure release, which may take 10 minutes. Release the remaining pressure. Serve and enjoy the cake once it is cool.

Thai Coconut Custard

Ingredients

- 1 cup unsweetened coconut milk
- 3 eggs
- 1/3 cup any sweetener
- 3-4 drops pandan extract

Directions

1. Mix together the eggs, milk, sweetener and the pandan extract, blend well and pour it into a 6-inch pan. Cover the pan with a piece of foil.

2. Pour 2 cups of water into the Instant Pot, place a trivet inside, and carefully place the pan on the trivet.

3. Close the Instant Pot, and set it to Manual mode, adjusting the cooking time to 30 minutes under high pressure.

4. Opt for the natural pressure release, which may take 10 minutes. Cool in the refrigerator until the custard is set. Serve and enjoy.

Chocolate Chip Pumpkin Cake

Ingredients

- 3/4 cup whole-wheat flour
- 3/4 cup all purpose flour
- A pinch of salt
- 1 tsp baking soda
- 1/2 tsp baking powder
- 3/4 tsp pumpkin pie spice
- 3/4 cup sugar

- 1 medium banana mashed
- 2 Tsp canola oil
- 1/2 cup Greek yogurt
- 1/2 cup pureed pumpkin
- 1 egg
- 1/2 tsp pure vanilla extract
- ½ cup chocolate chips

Directions

1. Take a medium bowl, add all the ingredients except the chocolate chips and mix well using a hand blender. Ensure the dough is soft and fluffy.
2. Switch on the Instant Pot, add about 2 cups of water and insert a trivet inside.
3. Now, take a cake pan which will fit the Instant Pot. Grease it with some butter or cooking spray, pour the dough and add the chocolate chips, mix well and set on the trivet.
4. Close the Instant Pot, and set it to Manual mode, adjusting the cooking time to 30 minutes under high pressure.
5. Opt for the natural pressure release, which may take 10 minutes. Cool in the refrigerator until the custard is set. Serve and enjoy.

Avocado Banana Plantain Cake

Ingredients

- 1 plantain
- 1/2 ripe banana
- 1/4 cup mashed avocado
- 2 tsp melted coconut oil
- 2 tsp honey
- 5 tsp cocoa powder
- 1/2 tsp apple cider vinegar
- 3/4 tsp baking soda
- 1/8 tsp cream of tartar
- 1 cup water
- Garnishes: coconut cream, coconut flakes, or fruits

Directions

1. Add the plantain, banana, avocado, coconut oil, honey, cocoa, vinegar, baking soda, and cream of tartar to a food processor and blend until smooth
2. Grease 3 small bowls with some cooking spray and pour the batter into the bowls until they are about ¾ full.
3. Pour the water into the Instant Pot and place the steaming rack inside. Place the bowls on the steaming rack.
4. Close and lock the lid. Press Manual mode, setting it to 20 minutes on high pressure. Once done, opt for the natural pressure release. Garnish with coconut cream, coconut flakes, or fruit and serve warm.

Pumpkin Pudding

Ingredients

For Pumpkin pudding

- 1/2 cup coconut milk
- 2 tsp gelatin
- 3/4 cup pumpkin puree
- 1/2 cup coconut sugar
- 1 pastured egg
- 1 tsp cinnamon powder

- 1/2 tsp nutmeg powder
- 1/2 tsp ginger powder
- 1/4 tsp clove powder
- 1/2 tsp allspice
- 1/2 tsp sea salt
- 1 cup water

For Coconut Glaze

- 3/4 cup coconut cream, at room temperature

- 1 tsp ginger powder
- 1 tsp stevia

Directions

1. Take a small saucepan and pour the milk, heating it on low heat. Keep stirring and gradually add the gelatin. Keep stirring until fully dissolved.

2. In a medium-sized mixing bowl, combine the milk + gelatin, pumpkin, coconut sugar, egg, spices, and salt. Stir well. Then pour this mixture into a jelly mold.

3. Add 1 cup water and place a steaming trivet into the Instant Pot. Place the pumpkin pudding on the trivet. Close the lid and set it to Manual mode on high pressure for 30 minutes.

4. Once done, release the pressure naturally, then carefully remove the bowl and allow it to cool under room temperature. After a while, put it in the refrigerator and cool it down for around 4 hrs and allow it to set.

5. In a small mixing bowl, add the coconut glazing ingredients, combine well using a hand blender.

6. Now, remove the bowl with the pudding from the refrigerator, garnish the coconut glazing and any nuts of your choice and serve.

Chocolate Pudding Cake

Ingredients

- 2/3 Cup chopped dark chocolate
- 1/2 Cup applesauce
- 2 eggs
- 1 tsp vanilla
- pinch of salt
- 1/4 Cup arrowroot
- 3 Tbsp cocoa powder
- powdered sugar for topping

Directions

1. Switch on the Instant Pot, add 2 cups water and place a steaming trivet inside. Now add the dark chocolate to a bowl and place it inside the pot carefully and select the sauté mode and allow the chocolate to melt.
2. Now add the applesauce, eggs, and vanilla in a small mixing bowl. Add the dry ingredients and slowly mix them in the cut and fold method.
3. Grease a 6″ cake pan with butter or coconut oil. Pour in the cake batter, and set the pan on the instant pot's trivet above the hot water.
4. Set the pot to Manual mode, adjusting the time to 5 minutes on high pressure. Opt for the quick pressure release.
5. Remove the cake pan from the Instant Pot and let cool for 10 minutes before transferring to a serving plate. Dust with powdered sugar and garnish with berries or nuts of your choice.

Biscuit Yogurt Cake

Ingredients

- 8 ounces Digestive Biscuits
- 10 fl oz Greek Yogurt
- 3 Small Bananas
- 1 Can Condensed Milk

- 3 oz Butter
- ½ Tsp Vanilla Essence
- 1 tbsp Caramel Sauce

Directions

1. Switch on the Instant Pot, add 2 cups of water, and place a trivet, then add the condensed milk into a bowl and place the bowl inside the pot carefully on the trivet.
2. Set the pot to Manual mode to 35 minutes on high pressure.
3. While the milk is cooking – take a saucepan and add the butter and allow it to melt .Crush the digestive biscuits and when the butter has melted add the biscuits. Mix well and add them to the bottom of your baking tin. Place it into the fridge to allow it to cool and set.
4. When the cooking time for the condensed milk is over, opt for a quick pressure release and carefully remove the condensed milk can and allow it cool for 30 minutes. Once it's cool, pour it in a bowl, add sliced bananas and mix well.
5. Now, take your crust from the fridge and pour the mixing bowl ingredients over the crust.
6. Refrigerate the cake for 4-6 hours.
7. When serving, add the vanilla and the yoghurt together and mix well and then pour it on the top.
8. Drizzle with caramel sauce and enjoy.

Vanilla Cheesecake

Ingredients

- 2 cups Cream Cheese
- 2 large eggs
- 1 medium vanilla bean scraped
- 1 tsp organic vanilla extract
- 1/2 cup Swerve Sweetener
- Red Raspberry Chia Jam

Directions

1. Take a large mixing bowl, add all the ingredients and insert a blender to blend the mixture well. Transfer to an 8-inch pan and cover tightly with foil.
2. Pour 2 cups of water in the Instant Pot and place the pan on top of the steaming rack.
3. Set the pot to Manual mode and adjust the time to 20 minutes cook under high pressure.
4. Allow the pressure to get released naturally. Remove the pan from the Instant Pot and cool down to room temperature for 30-60 minutes before chilling in the refrigerator.
5. Before serving, add the raspberry jam on top and enjoy.

Apple Crisp

Ingredients

- 5 chopped medium-sized apples,
- 2 tsp cinnamon powder
- 1/2 tsp nutmeg powder
- 1/2 cup water
- 1 tbsp maple syrup
- 4 tbsp butter
- 3/4 cup rolled oats
- 1/4 cup flour
- 1/4 cup brown sugar
- 1/2 tsp salt

Directions:

1. Add the chopped apples into your Instant Pot.
2. Sprinkle with cinnamon and nutmeg. Add the water and maple syrup.
3. Now, melt the butter in a small bowl.
4. Mix together melted butter, oats, flour, brown sugar and salt. Add the mixture on top of the apples. Close the lid of the instant pot.
5. Use the manual mode, and set it on high pressure for 8 minutes. Allow the pressure to get released naturally, then let the apple crisp rest for a few minutes while the sauce will thicken. Serve warm topped with ice-cream!

Three-layered Chocolate Cheesecake

Ingredients

- 4 tsp butter, melted
- 1 ½ cups chocolate cookie crumbs

CHEESECAKE FILLING

- 3 packages low-fat cream cheese
- 1 cup sugar
- 2 tsp cornstarch
- 3 large eggs
- ½ cup plain Greek yogurt
- 1 tsp vanilla extract
- 4oz milk chocolate
- 4oz white chocolate
- 4oz bittersweet dark chocolate
- Sugared cranberries

Directions

1. Select a 7-inch pan and grease it well. Stir the cookie crumbs and melted butter together and press evenly over the bottom and halfway up the sides of the pan.
2. Place the pan in the freezer to set.
3. Take a mixing bowl and add the cream cheese and using a hand blender, mix it until smooth, scrape the sides of the bowl and mix again. Add the sugar and cornstarch; continue scraping and mix the ingredients together on low speed until well-combined and smooth. Add the eggs, yogurt and vanilla and mix just until well-blended.
4. Divide the batter into 3 separate bowls, melt the milk chocolate in the microwave. Add it to one of the bowls with the cheesecake batter.
5. Repeat the same step with the white and dark chocolate and pour to the other two bowls as well.
6. Refrigerate the 3 bowls for 15-20 minutes so they will be more firm for layering.
7. Pour dark chocolate batter over the crust and spoon to form an even layer. Very carefully spoon the dollops of the white chocolate batter on top of the dark chocolate, gently smoothing over the top so the layers don't mix up. Repeat with the milk chocolate batter.
8. Add 1 cup of water to the Instant Pot and place a steaming trivet inside. Carefully place the pan on the trivet.
9. Close the lid and set the pot to Manual mode on high pressure for 45 minutes.

10. Let the pressure get released naturally which may take about 10 minutes. Remove the pan and let it cool for 10 minutes. Allow the cake to cool completely and then cover and place in the refrigerator. I would suggest overnight.

11. Before serving, let stand at room temperature for 30-60 minutes. Decorate with sugared cranberries and enjoy!

Chocolate Lava Cake

Ingredients

- 1 Tbsp granulated sugar
- 1/2 cup butter, cut into pieces
- 1 chocolate chopped
- 1 cup confectioner's sugar
- 2 eggs

- 2 egg yolks
- 1 tsp instant coffee granules
- 1 tsp vanilla extract
- 6 Tbsp all-purpose flour
- 1/4 tsp salt

Directions

1. Take 2-3 small cups or jars and coat them with cooking spray or butter.

2. In your microwave, melt the chocolate and butter in a medium-sized bowl for about 1 minute. Stir and repeat the process for another 15 seconds until the chocolate is melted completely.

3. Stir in the confectioner's sugar. Add in the eggs, yolks, coffee, and vanilla. Add in the flour and salt. Divide the batter between the prepared cups.

4. Pour 2 cups of water into the Instant Pot and place the trivet inside. Place the cups inside on the trivet. Close the Instant Pot.

5. Make sure the steam release handle is in the sealing position. Cook on manual for 9 minutes on high pressure.

6. Once done, opt for a quick release and open the pot. Remove the cups and carefully dab off any condensation from the surface. Dust the cakes with some powdered sugar. Serve warm and enjoy!

Caramel Popcorn

Ingredients

- 1 Cup Corn
- 2 Tsp Coconut Oil
- 2oz Butter

- 2oz White Sugar
- 3 fl oz Whole Milk

Directions

1. Switch on the Instant Pot and add the coconut oil and butter to the Instant Pot. Select sauté mode and allow the oil and the butter to melt.
2. Once melted, add the corn and stir well. Adjust the temperature of the sauté mode on the display settings to bring the temperature up to hot.
3. Wait until the mixture starts popping and then close the lid of your Instant Pot and wait until popping stops after a few seconds, which means the popcorn is ready.
4. To prepare the caramel sauce - add the sugar into a saucepan along with 2 teaspoons of water. Place it on the low heat and keep stirring until the sugar starts dissolving. Once it goes light brown, add the butter and allow it to melt, mix it in and turn the heat down to very low.
5. Then carefully start adding the milk until the sauce coats the back of your spoon which means, the sauce is ready. Let it cool.
6. Transfer all the corn into a mixing bowl and add the prepared caramel sauce and thoroughly coat the popcorn in the sauce. Place it in the fridge for a while and add the sauce again to coat and then serve.

Chocolate Mousse

Ingredients

- 3 egg yolks
- 1/2 cup Swerve
- 1/4 cup water
- 1/4 cup cocoa

- 1 cup whipping cream
- 1/2 cup almond milk
- 1/2 teaspoon vanilla
- 1/4 teaspoon sea salt

Directions

1. Take a bowl and add the yolks and start beating them.
2. In a large saucepan, add the Swerve, water, and cocoa and whisk until sugar is melted and cocoa is well mixed and combined.
3. Now, add the cream and almond milk to the pan and whisk to combine well. Let it heat but don't allow to boil, turn off the heat.
4. Then add in the salt and vanilla and mix well. Pour about a tsp of the warm chocolate mixture into the bowl with the eggs and whisk to combine. Then start pouring the rest of mixture and slowly keep mixing everything thoroughly.
5. Pour mixture into jars. Add 1 1/2 cups of water into the Instant Pot along with a trivet and place the jars on the trivet.
6. Close the lid and seal the pot. Select Manual mode, setting it for 6 minutes on high pressure.
7. Once done, opt for the quick release of the pressure. Remove the jars the pot using tongs. Let them cool on the counter and then refrigerate for 4-6 hours & serve.

Brown Biscuit Bread

Ingredients

- 1/4 cup white sugar
- 1/4 cup brown sugar
- 1/2 tsp vanilla
- 1/2 cup butter

- 2 packages of biscuit dough
- 1 Tbsp ground cinnamon
- 1 Tbsp powdered sugar
- 1 1/2 cups of water

Directions

1. Open the Instant Pot, add 1 ½ cup of water and insert the steaming trivet. Now take a clean zip lock bag and add the white sugar, cinnamon, and biscuit dough. Then shake and mix well until everything is combined.

2. Add this mixture into a pre-greased pie pan, and then place the pan on the trivet. Close the lid and seal the pot.

3. Set the Manual mode for 20 minutes on high pressure. Once the time is up, opt for the quick pressure release and carefully remove the bread pan from the Instant Pot.

4. Take a medium saucepan and start melting the butter, vanilla, and brown sugar.

5. Place the bread on a serving plate and drizzle with butter mixture and serve!

Peach Cake

Ingredients

- 2 cans Dove Peaches
- 1 box yellow cake mix
- 1/2 cup melted butter
- 1 tsp ground cinnamon
- Vanilla ice cream for topping

Directions

1. Switch on the Instant Pot and add 2 cups of water and place a steaming trivet.

2. In a mixing bowl, add the cake mix and cinnamon. Mix well. Pour in the melted butter and stir to mix well.

3. Continue mixing to get a firm dough. Pour the dough into a pre-greased pan which you're your Instant Pot. Place the peach slices on top.

4. Place the pan on the steaming trivet and close the lid. Set the Instant Pot to manual mode and adjust the time to 10 minutes on high pressure.

5. Release the pressure naturally, which will take about 10 minutes. Open the lid and let it set for 5 minutes to cool. Spoon onto plates and serve with a scoop of vanilla ice cream.

Lemon Pie

Ingredients

For Crust

- 1 cup graham crackers
- 4 tsp melted butter

For Lime Filling

- 2 egg yolks large
- 2/3 cup lime juice
- 1 tsp lime zest
- 1 can sweetened condensed milk
- 2 tsp sugar

Topping

- 1/2 cup heavy cream
- 1/4 cup sugar
- 1 tsp lime zest

Directions

1. Take a 7' non-stick pan and grease it well with butter or cooking spray and keep it aside. Take a blender and grind the crackers.
2. In a bowl, add the cracker crumbs with the melted butter, Combine well and press this mixture into the bottom and sides of the greased pan.
3. Freeze it while you start making the filling. Add the egg yolks and sugar to a bowl. Insert a hand blender and blend thoroughly until the mixture thickens. Now add the condensed milk and keep mixing.
4. Add the lime juice and zest. Mix until combined well. Pour this mixture on top of the prepared crust and cover the pan with aluminum foil.
5. Pour 1 cup of water in the Instant Pot. Place the steaming trivet inside. Add the pan on the trivet. Cover the lid and seal the pot.
6. Select manual mode and set it to high pressure for 15 minutes. Let the pie cool for 10 minutes before releasing the pressure.
7. Remove the pie from the instant pot after the pressure has been released. Refrigerate for 3-4 hours or until set.

For Topping: Take a bowl and add the whipped cream and sugar and beat well to a creamy consistency. Add to a piping bag and pour over the pie once you are ready to serve.

Pumpkin Pie

Ingredients

CRUST
- 1/2 cup crushed Pecan Sandies cookies
- 1/3 cup chopped toasted pecans
- 2 tsp melted butter

FILLING
- 1/2 cup light brown sugar
- 1/2 tsp salt
- 1 1/2 tsp pumpkin pie spice
- 1 beaten egg
- 1 1/2 cups packed pumpkin
- 1/2 cup milk

Directions

1. Grease a 6' inch non-stick pan and keep aside.
2. Grab a large mixing bowl and add the cookie crumbs, chopped pecans and butter and mix well. Spread the mixture on the bottom and the sides of the pan.
3. Place the pan in the fridge for about 10-15 minutes.
4. **For the Filling** - Take a large bowl; add the sugar, salt and pumpkin pie spice, egg, pumpkin and evaporated milk. Mix thoroughly.
5. Pour the above mixture over the pie crust. Cover the top of the pan with aluminum foil.
6. Add 1 cup of water into the instant pot, and place the steaming trivet inside. Place the pan on the trivet and lock the lid.
7. Select Manual mode, adjusting it to High Pressure 35 minutes. Once done, turn off the device and release the pressure naturally which will take 10 minutes.
8. Carefully remove the lid. Remove the pie and cool it the refrigerator for about 4 hours. Serve with whipped cream on top.

83574233R00069

Made in the USA
San Bernardino, CA
27 July 2018